Mexico

by Gina DeAngelis

Consultant:
Marisol Reyes
Mexico Project Coordinator
Georgetown University
Washington, D.C.

Blue Earth Books

an imprint of Capstone Press
Mankato, Minnesota

Blue Earth Books are published by Capstone Press
151 Good Counsel Drive, P.O. Box 669, Mankato, Minnesota 56002
http://www.capstone-press.com

Library of Congress Cataloging-in-Publication Data
DeAngelis, Gina.
    Mexico / by Gina DeAngelis.
    p.cm.—(Many cultures, one world)
    Includes bibliographical references and index.
    Contents: Welcome to Mexico—A Mexican legend—City and country life—Seasons in Mexico—Family life in Mexico—Laws, rules, and
customs—Pets in Mexico—Sites to see in Mexico.
    ISBN 0–7368–1534–1 (hardcover)
    1. Mexico—Description and travel—Juvenile literature. 2. Mexico—Social life and customs—Juvenile literature. [1. Mexico.] I. Title.
II. Series.
F1216.5 .D43 2003
972—dc21
    2002011584

Summary: An introduction to the geography, history, economy, culture, and people of Mexico, including a map, legend, recipe, craft, and game.

Editorial credits
Editor: Katy Kudela
Series Designer: Kia Adams
Photo Researcher: Jo Miller
Product Planning Editor: Karen Risch

Cover photo of Taxco, Guerrero, by Corbis.

Artistic effects
Corbis

2 3 4 5 6 08 07 06 05 04

Photo credits
Bruce Coleman, Inc./J. Sarapochiello, 18–19
Capstone Press, 23 (bottom); Gary Sundermeyer, 3, 21, 25 (both), back cover
Corbis/Randy Faris, 4–5; Keith Dannemiller, 8–9, 22–23; Danny Lehman, 10
   (left); Digital Stock, 14–15; Tom Bean, 15 (right); Chris Hellier, 27 (right)
Doranne Jacobson, 11, 13 (right), 29 (right)
Houserstock, Inc./Dave G. Houser, 16; Susan Kaye, 20
The Image Finders/F. Ziglar, 24
One Mile Up, Inc., 23 (top)
Patrick Batchelder, 28–29
PhotoDisc, Inc., 9 (right), 10 (right)
Photri Microstock, 26–27
The Viesti Collection, Inc./Joe F. Viesti, 6, 12–13, 19 (right)

Contents

See page 25 to learn how to make a paper bag piñata.

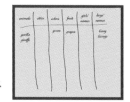

Turn to page 7 to find a map of Mexico.

Look on page 17 to learn a game many Mexican schoolchildren play.

Check out page 21 to find out how to make a Mexican treat.

CHAPTER 1

Welcome to Mexico

One of the world's oldest and largest stone monuments stands in Mexico. The Pyramid of the Sun rises more than 200 feet (61 meters) above the ancient city of Teotihuacan (tay-oh-tee-wah-KAHN). Thousands of years ago, an early group of people called Aztecs built this city.

Teotihuacan was once one of the largest cities of Mexico, but only its ruins remain today. People from around the world travel to Mexico to visit Teotihuacan and climb its pyramids.

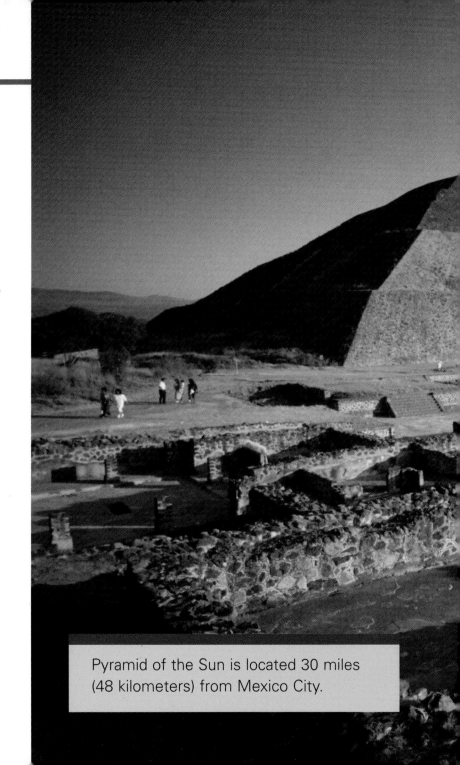

Pyramid of the Sun is located 30 miles (48 kilometers) from Mexico City.

Facts about Mexico

Name: ....Los Estados Unidos
........................Mexicanos, the United
........................Mexican States
Capital: ....Mexico City
Population: ....96 million people
Size: ....760,000 square miles
........................(1,968,400 square kilometers)
Language: ....Spanish
Religion: ....Roman Catholic
Highest point: ...Citlaltépetl, 18,700 feet
........................(5,700 meters)
Lowest point: ....Laguna Salada, 33 feet
........................(10 meters) below sea level
Main crops: ....Cotton, wheat, corn, beans,
........................tomatoes, coffee,
........................sugarcane, fruit
Money: ....Peso

Located south of the U.S. border, the country of Mexico is home to about 96 million people. More people live there than in any other Spanish-speaking country. Mexico's capital is Mexico City. Mexico City is the largest city in the world and the oldest city in North America.

About 24 million people live in Mexico City.

6

Map of Mexico

Laguna Salada

UNITED STATES

Baja California

Gulf of California

MEXICO

Gulf of Mexico

N

W   E

S

P A C I F I C
O C E A N

Teotihuacan ●
Mexico City ⬟
Puebla ●   ▲ *Citlaltépetl*

Cancún ●

Yucatán Peninsula

BELIZE

● Acapulco

GUATEMALA

Legend
⬟ Capital City
● City
ᴗ Lowest Point
▲ Volcano

CHAPTER 2

A Mexican Legend

Christmas is one of Mexico's favorite holidays. Mexicans fill their homes and churches with music and decorations. The bright red poinsettia plant is a popular Christmas decoration.

Poinsettia plants were first grown in Mexico. Some people believe the Aztecs found these plants. Others enjoy a popular Mexican legend told at Christmas. A legend is a story that is not completely true. The "Legend of the Poinsettia" tells how the plant became Mexico's Christmas flower.

At Christmas, people in Mexico decorate churches with poinsettia plants.

Legend of the Poinsettia

Long ago, a poor Mexican girl named María lived with her family on a small farm. Each Christmas, nearby villagers helped decorate the church. The children of the village made gifts to bring to church on Christmas Eve.

María was excited to make a special gift to set before the statue of Baby Jesus. María decided to weave a colorful blanket. But the yarn tangled. No matter how hard she tried, she could not weave the blanket.

When Christmas Eve arrived, María still did not have a gift. She told her troubles to her cousin Pedro as they walked to church.

"I do not have a gift for Baby Jesus," María cried. "I tried to make something beautiful, but I ruined it."

Pedro replied, "María, the Baby Jesus will love whatever gift you bring because it comes from your heart. Love is what makes a gift special."

The children in the legend were called María and Pedro. María was a young girl whose gift of love turned weeds into beautiful red poinsettia plants.

As they neared the church, María stopped to gather some green weeds. She took a ribbon from her hair and tied it around the weeds.

María joined the other children inside the church. The group watched as the priest placed the figure of Baby Jesus in the manger. The village children began bringing their gifts forward.

María looked around and saw all the people dressed in beautiful clothes. She felt very poor and ashamed of her gift. María hid the bunch of weeds under her shawl. She held back her tears and slowly walked to the front of the church.

People whispered as she passed them. When María reached the manger she said a quick prayer and pulled the weeds out from under her shawl.

People in the church shouted, "Look at the beautiful flowers!" María looked down and was surprised to see that each weed had bloomed into a bright red, star-shaped flower. All the weeds outside the church also bloomed.

The villagers believed María's love created a Christmas miracle. They called the poinsettia's red flowers "Flores de Noche Buena." The name means Flowers of the Holy Night.

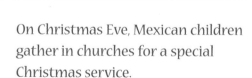

On Christmas Eve, Mexican children gather in churches for a special Christmas service.

CHAPTER 3

City and Country Life

More than half the people in Mexico live in large cities. It is easier for people to find jobs in the city than in the country. Some Mexicans leave Mexico to find jobs in the United States.

People live in many different types of housing in Mexico's cities. Some people live in large houses with a patio or courtyard in the middle. Some people live in high-rise apartment buildings.

People who cannot afford these types of homes may live on the edges of Mexico's cities. Their small huts do not have running water or electricity.

Many people in Mexico live in apartment buildings.

Some people in Mexico live in huts outside of large cities.

CHAPTER 4

Seasons in Mexico

Mexico's seasons are gentle and warm. Most of Mexico never gets cold enough for snow. During the winter months, many visitors from the United States enjoy Mexico's warm weather.

Tourists often visit Mexico's resort towns. Cancún is located on the Yucatán Peninsula. Acapulco is found on the southern coast. Mexico's coastlines are famous for their warm, sunny weather and excellent beaches.

Most of Mexico's large cities lie in the central part of the country. This region is

Cancún is known for its sandy beaches.
Many tourists visit this Mexico town
each year.

People in northern Mexico sometimes wear shawls
and jackets to keep warm. Temperatures there are
cooler than in the south.

15

located on high, flat land called a plateau. Central Mexico's warm climate is good for street merchants. They sell fruit, vegetables, and other goods year-round.

In most areas of Mexico, the weather is always mild enough for people to play outdoor sports. Soccer, called fútbol, is Mexico's favorite sport. Baseball is also a popular outdoor sport in Mexico.

People in Mexico can buy a variety of fresh fruits and vegetables all year.

Basta!

Mexican school children often spend their play time outdoors. But on a rainy day, school children can easily find indoor games to play. "Basta!" is a game Mexican children often play in their classrooms.

animals	cities	colors	fruit	girls' names	boys' names
gorilla giraffe		green	grapes		Gary George

What You Need

two or more players
a sheet of paper for each player
a pencil for each player

What You Do

1. Each player divides a sheet of paper into six columns.

2. Players write a category name at the top of each column. (For example, they may write animals, cities, colors, fruit, girls' names, and boys' names.)

3. A player starts the game by reciting the alphabet.

4. While the first player is reciting the alphabet, another player says "Basta!" This Spanish word means "Stop!"

5. The last letter of the alphabet to be spoken is the letter that all players will use for their first round of the game.

6. In each category, players must write as many words as they can that begin with the last letter spoken.

7. The player who recited the alphabet stops the game by saying "Basta!" All players stop writing.

8. Players read the words in their six columns. Players receive 100 points for each word or 50 points if someone else wrote down the same word. The highest score wins the round.

9. Players play several more rounds, keeping track of their points each round. The player with the highest overall score is the grand champion.

CHAPTER 5

Family Life in Mexico

Households in Mexico often are large. Most parents have three or more children. Grandparents, aunts, uncles, and other family members sometimes live in the same home.

Mealtime is an important part of family life in Mexico. On Sundays, many families enjoy a midday meal called a comida. The comida has several courses including soup, salad, rice and beans, and a main dish.

Mexicans eat tortillas with almost every meal. Tortillas are a round, flat bread made from cornmeal or flour.

Many Mexican families have three or more children.

Mexican Piñatas

Birthdays in Mexico are a time for family fun. People enjoy food, music, and games.

Young children often play a piñata party game. A piñata is usually shaped like an animal, a star, or even a carrot or other vegetable. Piñatas are filled with candy and toys. Children try to break open the piñata with a stick to get the treats.

Mexicans also celebrate saint days. Each saint in the Catholic Church has a feast day once a year. On a saint's feast day, Mexicans named after this saint celebrate the day as a birthday. On a saint's feast day, an entire Mexican town may also join together for a large festival called a fiesta.

For certain events, meals include mole (MOH-lay) sauce. The special spicy sauce comes in many different forms with up to 30 different ingredients. It often covers chicken or pork dishes. Some families even have their own secret mole recipes.

On Sundays, many Mexican families go to church before their midday meal. Almost all Mexicans are Roman Catholics.

The Holy Week of Semana Santa is one of the biggest holiday seasons in Mexico. Nearly all Mexicans celebrate this week, which lasts from Palm Sunday to Easter Sunday. Children do not go to school, and towns hold festivals.

On November 2, Mexicans celebrate Day of the Dead. On this day, people remember those who have died. Near midnight, families bring food, flowers, and candles to their relatives' graves.

Colorful statues are often part of Mexico's Day of the Dead celebration. People visit and decorate their relatives' graves on this holiday.

Cinnamon Oranges

Mexico is among the top orange-growing countries in the world. People in Mexico often include fruits in their dessert recipes.

What You Need

Ingredients
¼ cup (60 mL) powdered sugar
¼ teaspoon (1.2 mL) ground cinnamon
two oranges

Equipment
small bowl
dry-ingredient measuring cups
measuring spoons
spoon
knife
cutting board
plate

What You Do

1. Use a spoon to mix the powdered sugar and cinnamon together in a small bowl.
2. With the knife, cut both oranges into thin slices on the cutting board.
3. Arrange the orange slices on the plate.
4. With a spoon, sprinkle the sugar and cinnamon mixture over the orange slices.
5. Chill the plate of orange slices in the refrigerator for one hour before serving.

Makes 2 servings

CHAPTER 6

Laws, Rules, and Customs

Mexico's official name is Los Estados Unidos Mexicanos, which means United Mexican States. The country is divided into one federal district and 31 states. Each state has its own capital city and state government.

Mexico has a president. Mexico's president may serve one six-year term. If the president is unable to finish a term, Mexico's Congress names a new president. This person serves as president until the country holds an election. Mexican citizens age 18 or older may vote in these elections.

Elections are an important time in Mexico. Many people 18 years or older vote on election days.

Mexico's flag is divided into three blocks of color. Green stands for independence, white means hope, and red stands for union. The flag's center shows an eagle with a snake in its mouth. This image is Mexico's coat of arms. It comes from the Aztec legend of the founding of the city of Tenochtitlán. Mexico adopted its flag in 1821.

Mexican money is called the peso. Both coins and paper money are used. Coins have values of 5, 10, and 20 centavos, and 1, 5, and 10 pesos. Paper money has values of 5, 10, 20, 50, 100, 200, and 500 pesos.

Mexico's law says that all children must attend school from the ages of 6 to 14. Children in Mexico attend elementary school for six years. They also attend a middle school for three years. After middle school, some students begin working. Others go on to high school and university. Rural children usually go to school up to age 14 before beginning work on the family farm or at home.

Mexico's government recognizes several national holidays. Banks, post offices, and government offices close on these holidays.

Cinco de Mayo is one of Mexico's national holidays. This May 5 holiday marks the day in 1862 when the Mexicans beat the French at the battle in Puebla. Towns and villages celebrate with fiestas. Mexicans also gather for an Independence Day celebration on September 16.

Dancing is part of Mexico's Cinco de Mayo celebration.

Paper Bag Piñata

Piñatas are a feature at Mexican fiestas. Children take turns wearing a blindfold while trying to hit the piñata with a stick. When the piñata breaks open, all the children scramble to pick up the candies and small toys that fall out of the piñata. Mexicans believe that the child who breaks open the piñata will receive good luck.

What You Need

a small colored gift bag
candies
tiny toys
peanuts
tape
hole puncher
scissors

string
colored tissue paper
glue
colored markers
stickers
ribbons

What You Do

1. Fill a bag about halfway to the top with tiny toys, candies, and peanuts.
2. Fold the top of the bag down, and tape the folded top shut.
3. With a hole puncher, punch two holes in the middle of the folded bag top.
4. Loop a piece of string through the hole.
5. Tie a knot at the end of the string.
6. Cut strips of tissue paper to make fringe.
7. Glue pieces of tissue paper to cover the bag.
8. Decorate the bag with tissue paper, markers, ribbons, and stickers.

CHAPTER 7

Pets in Mexico

Birds are popular pets in Mexico. Many homes in Mexican cities have a canary or finch singing in a cage.

Families who live in the countryside keep birds as pets. Instead of using cages, they build small wooden houses outdoors. Birds use these homes to nest and lay eggs.

Cats and dogs are also common pets in Mexico. But crowded cities do not make good homes for these animals. Homeless animals have become a problem in large cities. Many cats and dogs roam city streets.

Birds are a favorite pet in Mexico.

Blessing of the Animals

The Feast Day of de San Antonio de Abad on January 17 is a special day for animals in Mexico. On this day, the Catholic Church allows animals to enter church buildings.

Mexicans decorate their pets and their livestock with flowers and ribbons and bring them to church for a blessing. This saint day is held in honor of Saint Anthony, the patron saint of tame animals.

CHAPTER 8

Sites to See in Mexico

Some of Mexico's famous sites are the stone pyramids built by the Mayan people. The Maya lived thousands of years ago in the Yucatán Peninsula. The stone pyramids they built still stand today.

Mexico City also draws many tourists. The central square called Zócalo is the second largest public square in the world.

Mexico is known for its artwork. Mexican painter Diego Rivera painted large murals. Visitors can see Rivera's most famous painting on the wall of the National Palace in Mexico City.

Diego Rivera's mural draws many visitors to the National Palace in Mexico City.

Artists in Mexico

Mexico is famous for its arts. Artists make jewelry and woodwork, and they weave rugs and blankets. Talavera pottery is also famous in Mexico. During the 1500s, the Spanish brought this pottery to Puebla, Mexico. Today's artists continue to make tiles, plates, vases, and bowls.

Words to Know

Aztec (AZ-tek)—a group of American Indians who lived in Mexico before Spanish people settled there

fiesta (fee-ESS-tuh)—a holiday or religious festival in Mexico

legend (LEJ-uhnd)—a story told to explain things in nature or to teach a lesson; legends often are based on facts, but they are not completely true.

Maya (MEYE-ah)—a group of American Indians who lived in Mexico and Central America hundreds of years ago

mole (MOH-lay)—a sauce made of spices and chocolate served with meat

patron saint (PAY-truhn SAYNT)—a person honored by the Christian church for leading a holy life

piñata (peen-YAH-tah)—a hollow, decorated container filled with candy; a person wearing a blindfold tries to break open a piñata with a stick.

pyramid (PIHR-uh-mid)—a structure that is big at the bottom and small at the top; many of the pyramids in Mexico have steps.

To Learn More

Alcraft, Rob. *Mexico.* A Visit to. Des Plaines, Ill.: Heinemann Library, 1999.

Dahl, Michael. *Mexico.* Countries of the World. Mankato, Minn.: Bridgestone Books, 1997.

Gresko, Marcia S. *Mexico.* Letters Home From. Woodbridge, Conn.: Blackbirch Press, 1999.

McCulloch, Julie. *Mexico.* A World of Recipes. Chicago: Heinemann Library, 2001.

Useful Addresses

Embassy of Mexico
1911 Pennsylvania Avenue, NW
Washington, DC 20006–3445

Embassy of Mexico in Canada
45 O'Connor Street, Suite 1500
Ottawa, ON K1P 1A4
Canada

Mexican Cultural Institute
2829 16th Street, NW
Washington, DC 20009–4204

Mexican Government of Tourism
405 Park Avenue, Suite 1022
New York, NY 10022–4405

Internet Sites

Track down many sites about Mexico.
Visit the FACT HOUND at *http://www.facthound.com*

IT IS EASY! IT IS FUN!

1) Go to *http://www.facthound.com*
2) Type in: 0736815341
3) Click on "FETCH IT" and FACT HOUND will find
   several links hand-picked by our editors.

**Relax and let our pal FACT HOUND do the
research for you!**

Index